# T'OLYMPICS

# LET IT BE KNOWN

THAT ON THE 14TH JULY NEXT THE COMMITTEE OF

# T'OLYMPICS

WILL BE OPENING THE GREATEST GAMES EVER SEEN IN

# THESE PARTS!

**Entry 1/- for Adults   3d for Children**

# ACCEPT NO SUBSTITUTIONS

IT HAS COME TO THE ATTENTION OF THE COMMITTEE
THAT SOME PEOPLE FROM LANCASHIRE HAVE BEEN
ATTEMPTING TO ORGANISE

# TH'OLYMPICS

**BUT THIS IS JUST A PALE SUBSTITUTE FOR**

# T'OLYMPICS

**ACCEPT NO SUBSTITUTIONS!**

AT THE BREWERY FIELD FROM 2PM

# SHARP!

# T'Olympics

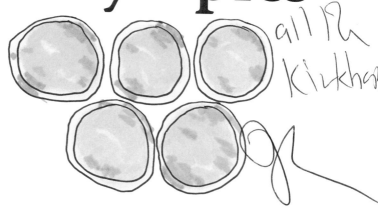

*To Grandma from all the Kirkham*

*compiled by*
**Ian McMillan**

*illustrated by*
**Tony Husband**

**Dalesman**

First published in 2011 by Dalesman
*an imprint of*
Country Publications Ltd
The Water Mill, Broughton Hall
Skipton, North Yorkshire BD23 3AG
www.dalesman.co.uk

Text © Ian McMillan 2011
Cartoons © Tony Husband 2011

ISBN 978-1-85568-292-4

Typeset in Stone Informal.

Printed in China by Latitude Press Ltd.

# Contents

# Introduction

*by*
*Professor Walt Blenkinsop*
*Department of Folklore, Cleckheaton University*

All the excitement around the London 2012 Olympics should be an opportunity to remember and celebrate the fact that the first Olympic Games of the modern era were held in Yorkshire in 1892, four years before the event in Athens which is commonly supposed to be the start of our current Olympic Games.

There are a number of reasons why T'Olympics, as they came to be known, have faded from public view.

Partly, it has to be said, they weren't very well organised, so that not a lot of people, even in Yorkshire, knew they were happening. Combine this with the theft of the gold medals (their discovery by Chutney the Whippet presaging the discovery of the stolen World Cup by Pickles the Dog years later), the fact that only three teams (Yorkshire, Lancashire and France) took part, the fact that many of the stadia remained unfinished even after the games, and the fact that the Provisional Wing of the Yorkshire Dialect Society insisted that the programme was printed in that version of the local tongue known as Deep Tyke which is only comprehensible to fifteen people in Mirfield,* and perhaps most crucially the fact that it happened during one of the worst summers this country has ever known.

However, for me T'Olympics remains a true highlight in Yorkshire's sporting and cultural history; it was a brave endeavour that almost succeeded against the odds and, but for a bit of rain, some unfathomable language, a paucity of entrants and the disappearance of some precious metal, this could have been Yorkshire's finest hour.

It weren't. Enjoy the book.

---

*Fourteen. Obadiah died since I wrote this. He died smiling — or 'greepin'' as Deep Tyke would have it.

# A note about the organisation of this book

*by*
*Sarah Grimethorpe*
*T'Olympics Official Historian, Department of Cultural Pondering, Cleckheaton University*

It's difficult to encapsulate the grand folly that was T'Olympics of 1892 in such a small book, and more thorough analysis will have to wait for the publication of my fifteen-volume work *T'Olympics: Regionality and the Pursuit of Corinthian Perfection*, which is due to be published by Dalesman Books in 2034 or thereabouts.

However, for now, this book will have to do. We've included a number of primary sources (newspaper reports, letters, contemporary accounts), a description of the various events, a number of items from the university's collection of songs and poems that were written about the time of T'Games, and the rare series of collectable cards that were produced later in the 1920s.

Feel free to wander through this book as you might through a Yorkshire dale; use it for enlightenment, delight, joy and a feeling that history had been unkind to a certain place at a certain time.

Please also feel free to order my fifteen-volume work *T'Olympics: Regionality and the Pursuit of Corinthian Perfection* for the pre-publication price of £234.78.

# T'Olympics Events

You'll find descriptions of some of t'main events in t'Olympics throughout the book.

Some events are lost, some events were planned but never happened (Team Winder Weshing, Pro-celebrity Knurr and Spel) and one or two were frankly deemed too dull for a volume of this intellectual depth. Yes, I'm thinking of 'Watching Whitewesh Dry'.

Why not try and recreate some or all of T'Events next time you've a spare afternoon? The publishers would be very pleased to see photographs of the results, particularly if comedy injuries are involved.

Enjoy T'Events. Remember: this is t' true spirit of T'Olympics: enjoyment.

# Beer Spilling

### *History of the event*

Beer spilling has a long and honourable history throughout the whole of Yorkshire. Historians speculate that when beer was first brewed by the monks of Brewfast Abbey near Ripon in the ninth century, it was in fact brewed to be spilled not supped, and that the first time beer was actually drunk it was because a monk accidentally sucked the edge of his habit as he bent down to shine the buckle on his left sandal.

Sociologists say that spilling beer over friends, foes, or in certain cases, yourself is a powerful bonding exercise as well as a fairly harmless way of establishing territorial rights.

In a sense it's more of an art event than a sporting discipline.

## How it is played

Two teams of Spillers line up opposite each other. Each team member is dressed in a white suit and white hat. The idea is to spill as much beer as possible over the opposition in a given time. Each team is then weighed and the one which tips the scales as the lightest wins, because they will have avoided the most beer as well as inflicting the most beer on the opposition.

The suits are then wrung out into buckets which are then glugged from until the early hours.

# Trouser-Hutching

**History of the event**

Even in the twenty-first century, the Yorkshire trouser-hutch is a common sight as the middle-aged to elderly man attempts to adjust his kecks, either over his belly, under his belly or around his belly. The result can be a kind of eyewatering tightness or the kind of low-slung effect mainly achieved by boyz in da hood.

Its origins go back centuries to the Hosiery Tax of 1256 which led to Yorkshiremen wearing the equivalent of secondhand tights which, of course, had to be hutched.

The main thing about a trouser-hutch is that it has to be done quickly to stop the people you're with ribbing you about it. This

has led to the totally unofficial street sport of Rapid Trouser-Hutching, which has in turn led to…

### How it is played

Ten men from each village don badly fitting trousers and stand in a line.

Seasoned players of Rapid Trouser-Hutching always say that this is the worst time, the waiting to hutch. As the trousers begin to slide downwards there's an almost unbearable need to hutch.

At a given signal (usually the simple shout of 'HUTCH!', although trombones are blown in certain villages, and in one hamlet near Leyburn a pair of giant trousers are paraded through the village and hutched with the aid of pulleys and winches), the team hutch their trousers as fast as they can. Only when their own trousers are well and truly hutched can they help others to hutch.

Such is the speed and dexterity of the hutchers that the event is often over in less than five seconds.

# Arguing and Sulking

*History of the event*

T'Committee of T'Olympics, in their search for truly Yorkshire Olympic events came up with the idea of an event based on two of the Yorkshire citizen's more popular pastimes, that of arguing and sulking.

It's well known that people from Yorkshire will argue at the drop of a hat\*. They will argue about who dropped the hat, whose hat it was that got dropped, where the hat dropped and how far, what kind of hat it was, how big the hat was and whether the hat dropper meant to drop or if it was just an accident. The argument finished, the loser

---

\*no they won't

As a spectator sport, I've seen better

invariably begins to sulk and can be left sulking for hours if not days.

Sadly for T'Committee, the event didn't turn out quite as planned.

### How it is played

Two teams of arguers line up facing each other*. At a given signal the first subject for argument is announced by the newly appointed Argument Starter, who shouts:

"Nobody has ever seen a red banana."

A fierce argument ensues, but only for a very short time as, after a couple of minutes of verbal ding-dong, the team begins to sulk one by one until both teams are engaged in major sulks that lead to immobility and a kind of hibernation. The event is abandoned.

*no they weren't

# Walter Brefton's Mesmer Ray

To: T'Committee, T'Olympics

26th April 1892

Dear Sirs,

   It has come to my attention that you are hoping to hold a Yorkshire version of the ancient Olympic Games in July of this year.

   May I introduce myself? My name is Walter Brefton from Sefton near Liverpool, and I have the peculiar and yet invaluable talent of being able to stop rain from falling by means of my Mesmer Ray.

Imagine, if you will, large number of athletes gathered for the games. The sun is shining and birds are singing. In the corner of the sky a small black cloud appears, like a beauty spot on an otherwise unblemished face. The athletes seem to be unconcerned. But look: the black cloud is growing. It is getting bigger! And bigger!

In the distance a rumble of thunder is heard and a bolt of lightning splits the sky. Raindrops the size of florins begin to fall on the athletes. Hailstones so large they have their own gravitational fields crash down on the unprotected heads of runners. Large puddles appear, quickly expanding into lakes and small inland seas. The games are a washout and have to be abandoned, costing the organisers (and I know this will pain you Yorkshire folk) a large amount of money.

Imagine, if you will, another possibility. The athletes are gathered. The sky is blue. The small dark cloud appears in the corner of the sky. The sky darkens. Walter Brefton appears with his Mesmer Ray. The Ray shoots Mesmer Particles and Froton-botons into the sky. The cloud retreats. The sky remains blue. There is no rain today.

Let me repeat: There is no rain today.

For a negotiable fee, the use of the Mesmer Ray can be yours throughout the duration of the games.

Think on my offer.

I remain,

Walter Brefton

# Collectable Cards

In the 1920s, interest in T'Olympics was revived after a musical, *Yorkies Running and Jumping*, was (briefly) popular at the Lyceum Theatre in London. There's more about the musical on page 142, but one spin-off of the musical was a set of T'Olympics cards which were manufactured in Leeds by Broomhilghe & Son and distributed with the *Yorkshire Thinker*, a weekly philosophical journal that could be said in many ways to be a precursor to the *Dalesman*.

The editors of this present volume have obtained (via Sneaky Pete McHugh's second-hand stall on the market — no questions asked) a set of the cards and they'll be appearing at intervals throughout the book.

# Mystic Mabel

Mystic Mabel, the self-styled 'Knaresborough Shaman', said, a month before T'Olympics started, and I quote:

"Summat amazing will drop from t' sky onto whoever won t' first medal of T'Games."

Mystic Mabel's predictions usually came true, although they were usually of a more general nature. Two years previously she had informed the world that Christmas would fall in December, and she had issued a warning to swimmers in the Nidd that "water was to be found in the vicinity of the river's banks".

Despite this, and mainly because of her knack for publicity, she was revered as a seer, so crowds gathered to see what would fall from the sky on the first day of the tournament.

The first game on the first day was the little-known sport of Hoop Cuckling, where a number of hoops had to be cuckled by a team of six (including, of course, one Raven-mester), and it was won, as expected, by Skipton St Walter's Chapel.

As the medal ceremony began, the eyes of the spectators shifted nervously from the podium to the sky to Mystic Mabel.

As the ceremony began, Mabel suddenly pointed to another part of the sky and shouted 'Look over there!'

Everybody looked and as they did so she took advantage of the distraction to hurl a model of an eagle into the air, which fell to the ground.

Sadly, given the unseasonably strong winds and the heaviness of the model which Mabel's husband Daft Jack had made in his shed, the eagle only rose three feet in the air before falling again.

A number of spectators saw the whole deception and Mystic Mabel was hounded out of town.

She never worked as a shaman or seer again, instead setting herself up as a professional wrestler, where she was known as Mighty Mabel.

# Letter from Alphonse D'Alphonse to T'Committee of T'Olympics

Felicitations to you all from that far shore of the mind that mere mortals call 'Art'. My name is Alphonse D'Alphonse and I am a painter, a dauber, a flicker of colour onto canvas.

But I am more than that. I can supply signed affadavits from King Wulf of Denmark, Chief Olouwole of the Zulus and Bert Hodge the Beer Millionaire that my paintings achieve the status of 'Art'.

Twice I have used that three-letter word and I beg your indulgence to be able to use that wonderful word once more.

I would die a happy man if I could be appointed the official artist of T'Olympics, creating works of art based upon the physiognomy of the athletes involved in the games.

I confess that I am not cheap. A canvas will cost you more than a hundred pounds. I confess that I am not what fools, philistines and knaves call a 'representative' artist; in short, I capture the essence of my subject in what I call The School of Few Dots.

Let me briefly explain FewDottism. Each canvas will contain three dots, sometimes in different colours, sometimes in the same colour. The dots will be small; some fools, philistines and knaves will call them 'insignificant'.

Let me reassure you that these dots will contain, if I may be so bold, the heart and soul of the athlete.

My terms are strictly cash on commission, paint and canvas extra.

Yours in Art,
Alphonse D'Alphonse
Artist

# Billy Mitherer, Egg Deliverer

Billy Mitherer kept an egg farm and was awarded the honour of supplying all T'Olympics athletes with eggs for the duration of T'Games. Unfortunately, due to Billy's clumsiness not one egg arrived whole at T'Olympic Site. Billy's excuses included:

Ah slipped.

Ah fell ower.

Bottom fell aht on't bag.

Bottom fell aht on t' sack I used instead o' a bag.

Bottom fell aht on t' box I used
instead of a sack.

Bottom fell aht on t' barrow.

I got nervous meetin' all them
fit folk and started ditherin' and
dropped 'em, like.

I got attacked by t' Omelette Boys.

Me mam told me not to put all me
eggs in one basket and I lost me
basket and so I couldn't transport
me eggs.

# T'Spirit on't White Rose

The organisers of T'Olympics wanted to personify t'Olympic ideal in a figurehead like Britannia or Boudicca or Helen of Troy.

They fixed on the idea (one of those ideas that the philosopher Joe Locke referred to as "a fifteen-pint-idea") of T'Spirit on't White Rose, who would be played by a girl from the local school. A pole-vault competition seemed the fairest and most obvious way to decide who should wear the crown, and the winner was Josephine Mason, aged eight.

A Spirit on't White Rose costume was designed and made by hand, and Josephine was paraded through T'Olympic sites on the back of a specially decorated cart.

Sadly nobody had realised that Josephine

# T'SPIRIT ON'T WHITE ROSE

was allergic to the shoddy that her costume was made of; after three minutes she swelled to fourteen times her normal size and began to float towards Selby.

It was thought that she would be lost at sea but she eventually made safe landing in a field near Hedon. As the farmer said:

"Ah thowt it were an angel, like. Till she landed on me head."

Josephine suffered no long-lasting ill-effects and in fact made a substantial amount of money giving talks about her ordeal all over the North for the next decade.

12th March 1894

FROM →**DUKE & SONS**←

HOSIERY MANUFACTURERS, WALSALL

To: T'committee, T'Olympics

Sirs,

It has come to our attention that you are planning to hold a 'sporting event' in July of this year which you are calling T'Olympics.

Surely you are aware that Duke and Sons have been manufacturing the Olympic Corset for the last thirty years? Surely you know that The Olympic Corset is the leading corset in the crowded supportive underwear field thanks to its unique 'Hold-You-Firm' elastic/whalebone/asphalt structure? May we respectfully suggest that

You desist from calling your event T'Olympics.
You pay us a sum to be decided for the use of the word Olympic.
You allow us to display images of the Olympic Corset on any advertising material you may produce.

We await your reply
Yours in restriction

Marmaduke Duke

# Coal Sculpting

### *History of the event*

Towards the end of the nineteenth century, at around the time of T'Olympics, coalmines were being sunk all over Yorkshire and, because of the time it took for the miners to walk back to the pit cage from the coalface, a new sport (or was it an art?) began to emerge.

Miners would pick up pieces of coal as they walked and one of their number, nominated in advance, would shout out a word or a phrase which would become the subject of a coal sculpture, carved in the piece of coal by the miners using a small chisel or a penknife. The one deemed to be the best by the time they arrived at the cage that took them back to the light was declared the winner.

It wasn't as though all the subjects were easy either. Subjects given have included 'Three Foxes on a Stoop', 'The Last Turkey in the Shop' and 'Irony'.

Some of the pieces are exquisite, and can be viewed at the National Coal Mining Museum near Wakefield.

## How it is played

Contestants are lined up in a fake pit bottom made of wood and canvas.

The command 'Ready to Chip' is given. The command 'Prepare to Sculpt' is given. The command 'Get mekkin'' is shouted.

At that moment the word or phrase they have to respond to is yelled from within a box by a short but loud-voiced woman.

The sculptors then sculpt as fast as they can as they walk to the finishing line, about half a mile away, and in semi-darkness.

## The controversy

The event was mired in controversy from the off.

When the stout but loud-voiced woman shouted "Our kid!" everybody began to, in the words of the popular song of the time, 'sculpt and scuttle'.

The first man to the finishing line, John Taylor of Wath-upon-Dearne, had sculpted what many agreed was an uncanny likeness of his younger brother Jim. The stout but loud-voiced woman objected, however, saying:

"This looks nowt like our Harry."

Taylor asked who Harry was and the woman replied:

"Our kid. And Jim is your kid."

Thus Taylor was disqualified on a technicality, and the winner was declared to be an untouched and unaltered lump of coal which nevertheless bore a passing resemblance to the stout but loud-voiced woman's brother Harry.

This is the only known occurrence of a sporting medal being won by a simulacrum.

# T'Olympics Official Song

## *by Hubert Bartram*

Oh the bodies and brains of Yorkshire folk
Are tuned to a high degree of excellence!
To some people we are just a joke
But to me those kinds of thoughts are just
    arrant nonsense!

CHORUS:
Oh, T'Olympics!
Greatest sporting thing we've ever done!
Oh, T'Olympics!
If the weather is kind then we'll besport
    ourselves in the sun!

---

*\*T' worst songwriter i' Yorksher.*

*T'Olympic Flame.*

Just gaze upon our athletic frames
As we run and jump and perspire
In t' magnificent Olympic Games
In our appropriate and locally
    manufactured sporting attire!

CHORUS

So gather round those who support
    the Corinthian Ideal
Of sport as the mirror of what those
    of a spiritual bent call the Soul
And if anyone suffers minor injuries
    they will be very quick to heal
And sporting excellence is our goal!

CHORUS

# The Stillness & Slowness League
## 8th June 1892

T'Committee, T'Olympics

Sirs,

May we wholeheartedly protest against the appalling junket of 'sport' and 'movement' to be held in your part of Yorkshire next month. As is well known (see Mr. John Greathead's article 'Sports can make you unhealthy' in the Journal of the Stillness and Slowness League) any movement or exercise can hasten death and illness by, in some cases, decades.

We at the Stillness and Slowness league contend that immobility and a sedentary existence are the best recipe for a long life. May we suggest an alternative series of 'Games' for your event? These could include

Sitting still

Sitting very still

P.T.O

*Lying down*
*Lying face down*
*Lying face up*
*Slouching Lolling*
*Extreme Lolling*
*Extreme Lolling with Slouching*
*(NB: Only to be attempted by the*
*fully trained)*

*Should you wish to take this*
*further we would be very happy to*
*arrange a meeting with you although*
*of course you would have to visit us*
*as we don't move very far at all.*

*Yours in Sloth,*
*The Stillness and Slowness League*

# Great T'Olympics Medal Winners

## *Frank 'Chuck It' Muldoon*

Frank Muldoon was the surprise winner of the ale-chucking competition at T'Olympics.

The secret with ale-chucking is not only to chuck the pint pot of ale a great distance but also to chuck it in such a way that none of the ale is spilled.

Most chuckers can manage the chucking but not the non-spilling; the distance can be huge but if there is no ale left in the pot then the chuck is considered void.

Frank explained his technique by comparing the chucking of the ale-pot to the throwing of a discus.

"T' pot's got to spin," he explained at the press conference after his event. "T' action o' t' spinnin' makes t' ale stick to t' side o' t' pot."

A dunna mind thee chucking hy ale, frank, but leave mine alone

"Gravitational pull?" an interviewer asked.

"No thanks, I've just had me dinner," replied Frank, who then proceeded to glug ale from a glass.

# Synchronised Tea Supping

### *How it is played*

This is a team event, divided into male and female sections.

Each team consists of four Suppers and a captain or Poury Person. Teams sit at a table with cups and saucers in front of them.

At a given signal (usually the cracking of a biscuit in two) the Poury Person pours the tea into the cups. Points are given if no tea is spilled and if the sound is, to quote the rules, "the classic sound of pouring tea".

The four Suppers must then say, in unison and if possible in harmony:

"By, I'm ready for this cuppa, tha knows..."

They must then raise the teacups to their mouths. They must sup. They must slurp.

They must take biscuits and dunk three times, saying in unison and if possible in harmony:

"There's nowt better than a lovely biscuit, tha knows…"

They must then, if they're men take off their flat caps, and if they're women take a handkerchief out of their handknitted cardigan sleeves, and waft the cup of tea with the cap or handkerchief, saying in unison and if possible in harmony:

"By, it's a bit warm for me, tha knows…"

They must then sup and slurp again before laying the cup on the saucer and sitting back in satisfaction, saying, in unison and in harmony if possible:

"Eeeeeeee…"

As this is happening, judges with magnifying glasses are studying the teams to make sure that they are, in fact, doing everything at the same time. A finger a fraction of an inch out of place, or a crumb that doesn't drop from the biscuit at the same time as the other crumbs drop, can lose you valuable points

and may in fact cause the team to be denied a medal.

The winners can truly be said to be the best Synchronised Tea Suppers on the planet.

### The Malton Tea Team scandal

At the 1892 Olympics it seemed that one team would sweep the board with the medals; the team from Malcolm's Tea Emporium in Malton were streets ahead of every other group of synchronised suppers.

Those who had watched them practise spoke in awe and hushed tones of the military, almost impossibly precise way in which they supped, dunked, and spoke. When other teams had tired of repeated rehearsals and gone to the pub to finally drink something other than tea, the Malton Team had gone on and on.

One man, James Cridlas, a junior reporter on the *Malton Gazette*, became suspicious. Let him take up the story.

'I noticed that none of the Suppers or the Poury Person ever seemed to take a rest and, although they drank lots of tea, they didn't appear to eat or need to go anywhere to relieve themselves.

"When everyone else had gone home they carried on training, and so I pretended to leave but hid behind a wall to see if anything suspicious was going on.

"They were still going through the tea-drinking motions but then one of them, the Second Supper as he is technically known, began to drink much more slowly than the others and he dunked his biscuit as though in a dream. I then heard a terrible groaning sound and smoke billowed from the back of the Second Dunker's head. I let out a harsh cry and watched in horror as the Second Dunker went up in flames. Malcolm, of Malcolm's Tea Emporium, ran across the yard and doused the flames with a blanket. He saw me staring and began to weep.

Over a cup of warm milk in his Tea Rooms he told me the truth: his team were Automata, robotic devices created in his secret laboratory in the cellar under the kitchen.

"He explained it all to me: 'The gold medal would have been within my grasp; I knew that mere humans would tire, especially in the area of the biscuit-dunking arm. But my Tea-bots would never tire, and I would be remembered as the man who brought gold back to Malton.'

"I told him that I'd have to tell the relevant authorities and, somewhat surprisingly, he didn't seem to mind.

"He told me he was working on a new invention, that would revolutionise the way we communicated with each other; he called it the Yorkshire-net and I didn't really under-stand it, but it involved sending messages through space via the medium of something that sounded like a rare herb: cyberspice, he called it. It'll never catch on."

# A Training Session* by the Holmfirth Donkey Stoning** Team

Reyt! Av yer all got yer stooans? Reyt! Grip 'em! Grip them stooans!

Mavis: grip it like yer grip yer pint pot! James: grip it like yer grip yer cakes wot yer like ter chomp!

Reyt! Nar bend ovver t' step! Reyt ovver! No messing! No half-bendin'! Let me hear them joints creak! Let me hear them joints crack! Good! Yer doin all reyt.

Nar get guin! Get guin on that step! Stooan

---

*The session was, of course, conducted in Deep Tyke so may be unfathomable to most.
**This, of course, refers to the act of cleaning one's front step with a donkey stone and not the practice of stoning donkeys.

No, thas got t'wrong idea!

EEE AW
EEE OW!!

it! Come on! Stooan it! Stooan it and stooan it and stooan it sum moor! I wannt it gleeamin' and shiny and sparklin' and dazzlin'!

Doreen: dun't loise thi grip! Pete: wot's up wi thi? Tha tired? Tired? Tha can't be tired: wiv not started on back step yit, lad!

# Speed Weather-Grumbling

### *History of the event*

The nineteenth-century philosopher Paul 'I Dunno' Misterton noted in his 1823 book *The Yorkshireman: His Ways of Thinking* that:

"...the main preoccupation of the Yorkshire person is the 'sport' of grumbling about the weather. If it is warm, then it is too warm; if it is chilly then it is, to use the vernacular, 'flipping freezing'; even on a still, calm day with a few innocuous clouds in the sky, the Yorkshire denizen will complain that 'it's a still, calm day with a few innocuous clouds in the sky'..."

The book had a great measure of popular success, particularly in Lancashire, Derbyshire, Nottinghamshire, Lincolnshire and Cheshire.

The organizers of T'Olympics, one of whom was related to Misterton, came up with the idea of trying to include Weather Grumbling in the games. It was decided to subject teams to artificially induced weather conditions and work out which ones came up with the most inventive grumble.

A side-effect of the event happening at T'Olympics was to clear the streets of urchins, as we'll see later.

### How it is played

Teams of three Grumblers, consisting of a Chief Grumbler and two Grumblees, stand at the end of a covered walkway.

At the cry of 'Time for Weather' they begin to run down the walkway, and are subjected to different weather conditions.

They pass a fire stoked by urchins, to represent Extreme Heat. They have blocks of ice thrown at them by urchins, to represent Extreme Cold. They pass a steam engine, and the steam is wafted at them by urchins, to represent Fog. Then small stones are thrown

at them by urchins to represent Hail. And finally buckets of water are thrown at them by urchins to represent Rain.

At each Weather Station, as it's known, Listeners drawn from sharp-eared sections of the community (gossips, priests, librarians) are on hand to catch the grumbles, and the grumbles deemed the most inventive are given medals.

Examples of inventive grumbles include:

"By, it's hotter than my grandad's vest, and stinkier an' all!"

"By, this fog tastes like my mother's tea!" and

"What a day! Evicted from me house, broke me leg, and now — hail!"

# The Lancashire Ambassador

Noah Thornhill, the Lancashire Ambassador (embassies in London, Paris, New York and Kippax), was invited to T'Olympics as a matter of diplomatic courtesy, along with ambassadors from a number of different countries. Thornhill was the only one to turn up, and so, through gritted teeth, T'Olympic Committee had to treat him to a slap-up dinner at the town hall.

The collectable card depicts the moment when Thornhill, under the influence of quite a large volume of Yorkshire ale, attempted to alter (some would say deface, some would say redraft) the official banner of T'Olympics to read, in the Lancashire style, Th'Olympics. He was thwarted in his vandalism (some would

say improvement, some would say artistic endeavour) by the Batley Tug Of Whippet team.

# The Anarchist Threat

Just a week before the start of T'Olympics, T'Committee received a rather disturbing letter which we reproduce in full below:

Dear Sirs,

My name is Professor Hans Pfrczrbrno. I am Emeritus Professor of Linguistics and Politics at the University of Ramsbottom (Rawtenstall Campus). I hope you will forgive the intrusion of a Lancashireman on your White Rose event but I have important and disturbing news for you.

Here are some words, some phrases. Study them, and tell me what you make of them:

'Mystic Lop'
'Spicy Molt'

'Cot Simply'
'Comply Sit'
And, perhaps most disturbingly,
'Clot I'm Spy'
And
'Scot Lip My'

Do you see? Do you understand? Look again; look carefully at the words, nonsensical and absurd as they may appear to be.

Yes. Now you begin to see: all those phrases are anagrams of T'Olympics.

Now, one or two of them can be dismissed as what we Linguists call Trashagrams: in other words they have no real meaning. I would place Cot Simply and Spicy Molt in that category.

But what of Comply Sit? What of Clot I'm Spy and Scot Lip My? Ah yes, now I see that I have your attention.

It is my belief that in the very fabric of the name of your games one of your number has placed an anagrammatic call-to-arms to a number of anarchist groups working in your area, and in particular the two anagrammatic

We've taken the anarchist threat very seriously, I will now work Sundays too

anarchist groups China Tsar and Inca Trash. (Work it out for yourselves, dear members of T'Committee.)

Clot I'm Spy suggests that there are more anarchists in your ranks; Comply Sit is a hidden signal to those who would infiltrate your committee meetings; and Scot Lip My is perhaps a guarded indication that you should watch out for Hamish McFamish, the one Scot on your committee.

You have been warned!

Yours truly,

Hans Pfrczrbrno

(a name with no known anagram)

# Rhubarb Forcing

*History of the event*

An area of West Yorkshire around Wakefield, Lofthouse and Morley is known as the Rhubarb Triangle. Within this area you can find a number of the long, low buildings known as forcing sheds where rhubarb is grown in the dark; indeed they do say that, if you're very still and quiet, you can hear the rhubarb cracking as it grows.

A couple of years before T'Olympics, a group of local lads decided to try and scare Lady Thompson, who lived in Lofthouse Hall and who had a huge bed of open-air rhubarb on her front lawn.

"I've never seen the need for forcing sheds," she once told a reporter from the local paper,

"I consider that I can grow fine rhubarb just as well in the open air."

So the lads tunnelled under her rhubarb beds and then  forced sticks up through the ground as Lady Thompson was having her tea. One of the miscreants shouted through a homemade megaphone:

"Force us, my lady! Force us!"

Controversy ensured when Lady Thompson shot at the rhubarb with the gun she always kept by her side. Rest assured the lads never bothered her again, but the incident passed into local legend and the idea of T'Olympic event was born.

### How it is played

Players are each given six sticks of rhubarb to clutch. They are then lowered into a hole in the ground, from where they are directed into a tunnel immediately below the forcing field.

At a given signal (usually a loud blast on rhubarbophone, a kind of primitive trumpet) they try to force the rhubarb through the earth to the outside air, mimicking the actual action

of rhubarb growing, as though viewed in a speeded-up film.

The winner is the one who can force his or her sticks of rhubarb through the ground in the shortest time.

This event demands a number of skills of the participant: strength, to push the rhubarb stick through the earth; dexterity, to stop the stick cracking and breaking; and hand-eye co-ordination, because any sticks dropped on the floor of the tunnel incur a points penalty.

Participants are allowed to try and put each other off, either verbally by shouting things like "Watch out! I've just seen a spider the size of a parasol!", or "T' roof's coming in! Scuttle, pal, scuttle!", or "Does tha know, I think we've come on t' wrong day. Let's go home and come back termorrer. You first.", or physically by grabbing an opponent's rhubarb stick and forcibly breaking it or, in extreme cases, eating it.

ry and put the other teams off: pull faces, shout 'GERRART', make motion of hand across neck as though slitting a throat.

Accidentally place bricks or large pieces of wood in the opposition's buckets.

Glue their buckets to the ground.

If the event is on a Wednesday, tell them it's against the law to carry milk in a bucket on a Wednesday. Vary day to suit. (Cyril, I'll go through this with you later on a large piece of paper, so there's no need to worry.)

Grease their bucket handles.

Swap their milk for beer and encourage them to sup it.

Tell them as they arrive that the event has been called off due to a lack of milk/buckets teams/referees.

Tell them it's silk not milk unless they've got some silk.

Distract them and nick their buckets or their milk or both.

*List of tactics from the 4x100 yards Milk-in-a-Bucket Relay Team from Castleford, discovered in their training camp at the White Horse.*

# T'Strange Event

From the journal of the amateur scientist Cardew Craven:

Friday July 20th

As I was working in my laboratory on my Time Tricycle, the nodes on the end of my Gresham Generator began to glow. I constructed the Gresham Generator many years ago and, frankly, I've forgotten why or how, or indeed what, its purpose may be.

The glowing increased in brightness and intensity, and I turned from my Time Tricycle and went to investigate, and my heart leaped to my mouth and stayed there, massaging my teeth. A young boy stood in the centre of the Gresham Generator and I knew, somehow knew in the chambers that exist between the different nodes of your mind, that he had come from that uncharted territory known as t'future. I append a transcript of our conversation.

*Me:* Greetings. I will not harm you. Do you bring money?

*Boy:* Where am I?

*Me:* My laboratory. I am a scientist. I wish you no harm. Do you bring cash or valuables?

*Boy:* I don't know what you're on about. I were just sat there watching 4x100 metres relay, and then I went all wobbly and then I ended up here.

*Me:* What is this 4x100 metres that you speak of? And did you bring precious metal of any kind?

*Boy:* I was at the Olympics, and …

*Me:* T'Olympics? Our little festival of sport?

*Boy:* Eh? I mean the Olympics; London 2012.

*Me:* 2012? You mean the year 2012?

*Boy:* Well, that's what year it is.

*Me:* Not here it isn't. It's 1892 here.

*Boy:* I don't understand. You mean this is the past?

*Me:* It's the present I think. Do you bring jewels? Do people remember T'Olympics? Is our little part of Yorkshire famous?

*Boy:* Sorry, I feel a bit wobbly…

*Me:* Stop fading away! Leave the money with me! Leave the gold!

# Marathon Flat Cap Wearing in Extreme Heat

### *History of the event*

Dr Nathaniel Autumn, a surgeon working at Dewsbury Hospital For The Not Well At All, noted, in the hot summers of the mid-nineteenth century, that he was treating a number of middle-aged men for heat exhaustion and for the hitherto rare condition known as Extreme Cap Ring.

After a little investigation he discovered that the chief cause of these diseases and injuries was the refusal by staunch Yorkshiremen to take their flat cap off no matter how hot the weather was. As Dr Autumn wrote in *T'Yorkshire Medical Journal*:

"It seems that the male citizen of Yorkshire, once he reaches the age of fifty and above, will not remove his cap from his head under any circumstances. Because of this, and because all a Yorkshireman's bodily heat rises to the top of his head (unlike a Lancashireman's bodily heat which seeps out of the toes of his clogs), he can reach boiling point in seconds and the cap can become stuck to the skull as though soldered or glued, and when eventually removed for Christmas or for marital relations can cause extreme soreness and chafing."

Dr Autumn became interested in annotating how hot it would actually get before the cap would be removed, and he placed volunteer Yorkshiremen in greenhouses and next to large fires, and timed the eventual doffing of the cap.

### How it is played

This cap research would have remained in the scientific realm had it not been for Dr Autumn's brother, Philip 'Summery' Autumn, who had emigrated to America in the 1840s and had established a travelling circus all across the states of the eastern seaboard. He

returned to Yorkshire due to debt problems involving an elephant and a bearded lady, and was immediately taken up by the possibilities of Cap Wearing as part of T'Olympics.

He devised a course which went through various stages of heat, beginning via a series of matches held aloft by volunteers and working up through open fires and open boilers to what Philip described as "an incandescent wall of fire" produced by burning logs soaked in paraffin.

The competitor who could get to the end of the course and stand in front of the aforementioned wall of fire the longest was declared the winner.

The winner was George 'Asbestos Brain' Wilson who, incredibly, stood in front of the wall of fire for a week and a half. He had to be given his gold medal in a liquid state as it had melted during the event.

# T'Olympics Bard

Harry Green of Heckmondwike is commonly thought to be one of the worst poets Yorkshire has ever produced. His collections *Ah Wrote These Mesen* and *Ah Wrote These Mesen An' All* are prized by collectors of bad verse everywhere.

Green appointed himself as the official T'Olympics Bard, and one of his efforts is reproduced on the facing page. His verses were collected and published in *Ah Wrote These Abart T'Olympics*, but no copies survive after a guerrilla raid by a militant faction of the Heckmondwike Poetry Society on the shed where Harry stored them.

## Just Afoor T' Start o' a Race

All the runners in their shorts and shoes are all lined up
Hoping to win a medal or get their hands on a trophy, ie a cup.
There's a kind of tension in the air
As they prepare to run as fast as they can from a line just here
    to a tape just there
And break the tape with their face or their nose or their chest
To prove that of all the runners running in this running race
    they have run the running race the best.
But of course this race is like LIFE
It is full of STRIFE
And if you lose it cuts like a KNIFE
And if you win it is like getting married to your WIFE.
The runners are ready but where is the starting pistol?
Somebody has left it in his house in Bristol
So the start of the race will be delayed
So this poem will end before the race begins, I'm afraid.

# Great T'Olympics Medal Winners

## *Meg Mason, Champion Shouter-in*

Meg Mason holds the world record for shouting her kids in for their tea; her shout was so loud that her children once heard her when they were on a Sunday school outing to Bridlington and walked home, a trek which took three and a half days.

Meg's voice has a quality which vocal experts have described as 'carrying'; it's not particularly loud but it penetrates, as neigbours can testify.

"When she shouts 'Come in for your dripping!', my husband's ashes tremble in their urn on the mantelpiece," as Mrs-Dobell-next-door said.

She doesn't live next door: she lives two

doors down. She just happens to have an unusual name.

So it was obvious that Meg would win the
gold medal at T'Olympics. In fact she won the
gold, silver *and* bronze because she frightened
all the other competitors away.

# Curd Tart Tennis

### History of the event

Hilda Dawson of Selby was renowned for the heaviness of her curd tarts; no one ever worked out why they were quite so heavy but Hilda, a strapping and athletic woman, had to have the help of her husband Albert to lift them out of the oven.

A generous lady, Hilda would often make curd tarts for all her neighbours. Everyone enjoyed this on Engine Street, the terrace where they lived, apart from Brian Toulson at number 46, two doors away from the Dawsons. Hilda would deliver the curd tarts up and down the street, and Brian would throw his over the hedge, a considerable feat of strength and dexterity.

t'advantage t' big lass

Hilda couldn't believe that anybody wouldn't be delighted by her tarts, and so when Mr Toulson's tart flew through the air towards her garden, she batted it back with her shovel-like hands. Brian knocked it back again, Hilda returned it, and a rally could last for hours.

When suggestions were sought for events for T'Olympics, both Hilda and Brian (who had grown quite fond of each other over the years) suggested Curd Tart Tennis.

### How it is played

Real curd tarts are used, made to Hilda's secret recipe; a net is set up, made from an artificial hedge; and the game is scored just like tennis although, in an interesting linguistic variation, the word 'Custard' is shouted instead of 'Deuce'.

Line judges have to wear reinforced helmets because of the heaviness of the tart; a blow from one of them can cause amnesia, as George 'What's My Flipping Name Again' Morris found to his cost during the Selby Games.

# Stan, Stan, T'Olympic Man

If sporting mascots had been thought of at the time of T'Olympics, then Stan Stanley (otherwise known as Stan Stan) would have been the official mascot.

Stan loved everything about T'Olympics and believed, as he said "that T'Games will bring everybody together in a spirit of peace and harmony like sort of thing". He renamed his hovel T'Olympic Palace, and decorated it with the flags and banners depicting the five Yorkshire puddings which were the precursor of the modern Olympic symbol.

Sadly, Stan Stan attempted to tattoo the words 'T'Olympics for Peace and Harmony' on his own back using a series of mirrors and pulleys and sharp pencils dipped in ink. Due

to the extreme pain and the brandy he had supped to dull the agony, Stan Stan's spelling went awry and what he actually tattooed between his shoulder blades was the phrase 'T'Olunsics for Peas and Harms way', which meant that he was then too embarrassed to attend the events themselves, despite the fact that his mistakes could easily be covered up with a shirt. As he said, "I can see it, and that's what counts," even though he couldn't see it as the tattoo was on his back.

# The Kings Hotel

**CELEBRATORY MENU TO
MARK THE OPENING OF**

# T'Olympics

★ ★ ★

**STARTER'S ORDERS:**
SOUP OF ENDEAVOUR
WITH MEDAL-SHAPED BREAD ROLLS

**THE BODY OF THE RACE:**
SPEED SWEDES
MEAT YOU AT THE WINNER'S PODIUM
POTATOES IN IMPORTANT OFFICIALS'
JACKETS WITH MEDAL-SHAPED CARROTS

**THE FINISHING LINE:**
I SCREAM WITH EXCITEMENT AT
THE THOUGHT OF A MEDAL

Aye up... no Yorkshire pud?!
THE KINGS HOTEL Restaurant
Menu
Celebrate the opening

# SINGULAR RETRIEVAL BY CANINE DETECTIVE!

Following the news of the disappearance of all the medals for the forthcoming T'Olympics event to be held next week, members of T'Committee were despairingly engaged in attempting to fashion substitute medals from wood and puff pastry when one of their number heard a whining and a scratching at the door.

'Ah thowt n'moor on it' said Jennings Watson, a member of T'Committee. 'Ah thowt it were our Arthur. He often whines and scratches at't door when he's had a few days in't Dog and Duck and I usually don't let him in and he sleep's it off in't watter butt.'

Eventually, however, one of T' Committee members tired of the whining and scratching and flung open the door to reveal Watson's whippet Chutney clutching the lost medals in its slavering jaws.

'I were reyt thraphed!' Watson said, inexplicably. 'I can tell yer we gid Chutney a big booan to chew on that neet. After we'd spent several hours wrestlin't medals out on his chops…'

A happy ending, I think our readers will agree!

*Report from the Yorkshire News, 1st July 1892.*

# Mick Mason, Medal Artist

Before T'Olympics, Mick Mason of Methley was mainly known as a portrait painter.

For a few shillings he would go to the houses of the wealthy and paint them in oils. His trademark was what he called the 'Flatter 'em don't Splatter 'em' technique.

Before painting his sitters, he would ask them if there was any particular feature they wanted hiding or exaggerating. Thus none of his subjects ever had warts on their nose or a triple chin. On the contrary they often had perfectly shaped faces and eyes that shone like Flamborough Lighthouse.

He was also very careful not to spill paint on his sitters, after he was attacked in his early days as a painter by Lord Hoffley after azure

blue was discovered on his lordship's second favourite tunic.

Mick was set on by T'Olympics Committee to design T'Medals for T'Games. Mick's idea was that T'Medals should feature the part of the body that he considered the most important to any athlete: the lungs. Each medal would feature a competitor with a giant pair of lungs sprouting from his chest.

T'Committee were dubious but Mason was adamant. After T'Medals were struck, the Lord Mayor of Bradford made his famous remark that all but destroyed Mason's career:

"They look like they've got broccoli on their fronts."

This only partially accurate description made Mason a laughing stock in the (admittedly small) Methley art world, and he gave up the brush and returned to his previous occupation of bargee on the Methley Canal, sometimes painting the sides of barges — but only for his own satisfaction, never for a fee.

Mick Mason is one of the tragic figures of T'Olympics, and this card remembers him.

# NOTICE

## FRANKS PORK BUTCHERS

If you're coming to T'Olympics why not try
Our Gold Medal winning small pork pie!

It'll give you strength it'll make you sprint
It'll cure baldness and aid your squint!

All the competitors all agree
A Franks Pork pie is lovely with a nice cup of tea!

Before one of
Frank's Pork Pies

After one of
Frank's Pork Pies

# Peter Peter T'Olympic Hater

Peter Peterson, otherwise known as Peter Peter, was one of the few Yorkshire citizens who was totally against the idea of T'Olympics.

In his self-published pamphlet *T'Olympics: A Waste of Money if You Ask Me* he put forward the idea that the money spent on the games could be much better spent on Peterson's pet project, a tunnel linking Yorkshire with London.

T'Tunnel would, he argued, be quicker and safer than roads, which he suggested "were subject to the vagaries of the English weather", and canals into which "you might slip and drown".

As a measure of his protest he sealed himself up in the first five yards of T'Tunnel. After about half an hour everyone forgot about him but he was discovered three days later when members of T'Olympic Tunnelling teams found him.

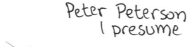

Even then, he wouldn't accept that if it hadn't been for T'Olympics he would have been entombed forever. As he wrote in his subsequent self-published pamphlet *Three Days Underground with only a Pocket Watch and a Spoon*:

"I would have dug my way out eventually. The spoon was a sharp one..."

I say, hast thou heard what those Yorkshire types are up to now? Well, I'll go to the foot of our stairs if they're not organising their own version of the ancient Greek Olympic Games!

I know, staggering isn't it? Picture a slag heap instead of Mount Olympus and a pair of pitman's clogs instead of the shoes of fire of Hermes, Winged Messenger of the Gods!

Yes, those Northern types will be running and jumping and throwing things like, as they would say up there, 'good 'uns'.

But I have just one question: what on earth will they use for their medals?

Why, coal, of course! Yorkshire is full of the stuff! Instead of Gold, Silver and Bronze medals they can win coal, coal and coal!

Except they call it Coyl! Coyl, coyl and coyl! And the games will coil around the Coylfield for at least a week.

And that's a lot of Coyl!

'Humorous' column from Punch, June 1892.

## Two Southern Toffs Watching T'Olympics

*1st Toff* – "I Say, Alfonse … What These Yorkie
Types Will Do for a Lump of Coal."

*2nd Toff* – "Makes You Larf, Don't It, Bertie."

# Getting Thyssen up Them Stairs

## *History of the event*

Getting sent up them stairs is a common occurrence for Yorkshire children. At the slightest misdemeanour an enraged Mam will shout:

"Get thyssen up them stairs now! And don't come back down till you've learnt some manners!"

## *How it is played*

Teams of four players, representing children, begin at the foot of a set of specially constructed stairs. These stairs are higher, steeper and more rickety than normal stairs.

At the shout of "Gerrup Theer!", the team has to climb the stairs as fast as they can despite their height, steepness and ricketiness.

Competitors describe the event as like "running straight up a cliff or a brick wall" and despite its brevity (think of a hundred-yard sprint vertically) it tests athletes to the limit.

# MISS TAIT'S DANCING SCHOOL

## PROGRAMME FOR THE OPENING OF T'OLYMPICS

**09.00:** THE MORNING SUN OVER T'OLYMPICS: UNDER 5s

**09.30:** A MARATHON IS RUN: UNDER 6s

**10.00:** SOLO: WHERE IS MY MEDAL
(LIGHT COMEDY) YVONNE BINNS

**10.15:** RUNNING AS FAST AS WE CAN: UNDER 7s

**10.45:** SOLO: YES, BUT WHERE IS MY FLIPPING MEDAL?
(DRAMATIC) YVONNE BINNS.

**11.00:** JUMPING HIGH, JUMPING LONG (UNDER 9s)

**11.15:** PUT THAT BLOOMING MEDAL DOWN, IT'S MINE!
(MELODRAMATIC) YVONNE BINNS AND
NANCY DYSON

**11.30:** OH I AM RUNNING SO FAST! (UNDER 10s)

**11.45:** NOW WILL YOU GIVE ME MY FLAMING MEDAL,
(EPIC, WITH METAL PROPS) YVONNE BINNS AND
NANCY DYSON

**12.00:** OH THE HAPPY HAPPY GAMES (UNDER 11s)

**12.30:** HOW FAR IS IT TO THE HOSPITAL?
(PERAMBULATORY, WITH EMOTION) YVONNE
BINNS AND NANCY DYSON

# The Terrible Mistake

On the day before T'Olympics were due to start, a carriage drove up to the organisers' hut and a stout man got out. He was wearing a top hat and a cape, and a monocle which glinted in the Yorkshire sun.

He was followed out of the carriage by an even stouter man carrying what looked like a tea chest because it was in fact a tea chest.

The monocled man removed his monocle and shouted, to the world in general:

"I'm here for my gold medals!"

As he did so, the stouter man ripped open the tea chest and flung loose tea in the air, where it hung momentarily and then floated towards rows of washing hanging in the back yards of myriad terraced houses nearby.

# THE TERRIBLE MISTAKE

The organisers of T'Olympics rushed out of the hut and stood in front of the monocle gent.

"What exactly are you here for?" one of them asked, his voice trembling like a tea leaf.

"Why, the Tea Olympics!" the man shouted and his companion flung more loose tea in the air, prompting a shout of "Will tha stop that nah!" from a terraced street a few hundred yards away.

"My Orange Pekoe will medal like heck!" said the man, taking off his top hat to reveal a pate as shiny as a mirror. "My Lapsang Souchong is a marathon not a sprint!"

I'll leave you to guess the rest: the terrible humiliation/the laughter behind sleeves/the arguments during which the monocle was thrown to the floor/the sad retreat in the cart/the tea-stained washing…

# Fishin' Wi' a Stick an' Some String an' a Pin

## *History of the event*

Fishing in local streams with a crude fishing rod made from a stick and a pin has long been a pastime amongst Yorkshire youngsters.

In the end, the catching of the fish doesn't really matter: it's the fun of making the rod from the stick and the string, and then bending the pin that counts.

T'Olympics committee planned to put a stop to all that by turning it into a highly competitive event.

## *How it is played*

Competitors have to line up and run a mile to pick up their stick. They then have to run another mile to pick up their string. They then

It's the wife,
thron her back!

have to run another mile to pick up the pin. They then have to bend it with their teeth and affix the pin to the string and the string to the stick whilst blindfold; they then have to run another mile to the pond, which is an artificial one built in the grounds of Lord Fitzpatrick's mansion.

Several of the poor of the village have to dress as fish and these were the ones that the competitors had to catch.

### The aftermath of the event

The event was not a great success because a number of the competitors dropped out after the first mile. The paupers playing the fish got fed up and went to the pub. The pond had been badly designed and most of the water trickled out hours before the event was scheduled to begin.

# The Legendary Abandoned Event

A Mr Martin Gainsborough came up with the idea for an event for T'Olympics which he said would be so popular that it would take its place in the pantheon of organised sports alongside recently developing games like football, cricket and rugby. He called the event T'Game and presented the rules and conditions of play to T'Olympics Committee.

Sadly for the game and for posterity Mr. Gainsborough presented the idea in such an impenetrable Yorkshire dialect that even the seasoned Yorkshiremen on t' Committee couldn't make out a word. Maybe you can help; here's the opening of his peroration:

"Reyt. T'Game'z like this tha sees. Gerra mell. A big'n — icklemells is ner gud. Tek thi mell an rubber it. Rubber it wi a clart else a parrot. Semmaz a biggun if tha can. Flit it. Jock it. Wi' t' ball tha munt coz if that duz tha'll gerrem docked. Points, tha knows. One deeper. Two scletty. Gerrit?"

# Y'Olympicf of 1292

Eccentric local historian Gordon Johnson shocked T'Committee of T'Olympics when he attended an open meeting during the planning of the games and informed them that, in fact, a similar event had been staged in the Middle Ages.

According to Johnson, Y'Olympicf were held in the exact same spot six hundred years earlier and his contention was that T'Committee should mark the event in some way.

He said that events held that year included Turnip Flinging, Ye Jumping of Ye Bladder, Ye Climbing of Ye Hill of Dung, Porridge-bucket Relay, Snake Chess and Peasant Belabouring (team and individual).

However, when pressed to provide proof of

the existence of Y'Olympicf, Johnston ran from the room in a state of high dudgeon, claiming a prior appointment with a baker of large pies.

# Getting a Good Wesh

Before the event begins, the competitors are covered in coal dust, steel shards and mill detritus. They are then led to a set of sinks where they must get what generations of Yorkshiremen have called "A wesh. And I mean a good wesh. And I mean a reyt good wesh."

This involves stripping to vest, gathering loads of water in the cupped hands, lathering with Pit Head Baths soap and rubbing the hands on the face and going

**Grbfrbrfrshhhhhhhhhh!**

Medals are awarded for the cleanest face, the lather furthest in your inner ear and the loudest

**Grbfrbrfrshhhhhhhhhh!**

# Saint Derek of T'Olympics

Any kind of gathering draws odd people to it, and 'Saint' Derek Wooton was certainly one of the odder people in the orbit of T'Olympics of 1892.

Derek had been a hermit from the age of sixteen, when his mother had decided that he was 'too delicate' for work on the family farm. Over the years he had lived in a series of caves and huts, and had become convinced that he was a saint.

When it was pointed out to him that you don't just become a saint, you have to be made into a saint, he replied that he was beatified in a secret ceremony in Hebden Bridge. When quizzed on how secret the ceremony was, he said "Well, nobody was looking".

When T'Olympics began, Derek turned up on the first day dressed in druidic robes and carrying a rusty handbell. He announced himself as 'Saint Derek of T'Olympics' and said that he was ready to offer spiritual guidance to anybody who needed it.

That afternoon he was approached by one of the Tong Parkin Baking Team, a gentleman by the name of Orville McHugh. McHugh confessed to Wooton that he had in fact cheated in the heats, using mixture he had prepared earlier, and he wondered if St Derek could absolve him of his Parkin Sin.

In a move that could have been predicted by anyone with an ounce of wit (which of course left Orville out of the equation), 'Saint' Derek said that he would be able to give absolution but would require a deposit of £20 for what he termed vaguely "spiritual instruments and soul compasses".

McHugh paid up, and of course Saint Derek disappeared and only returned four months later, three stone heavier with a tattoo and shaking hands.

As McHugh said later, "You live and learn" — which in his case was untrue as he was subsequently declared bankrupt after spending all his savings on buying shares in a coal mine on the planet Uranus.

# The Royal Visit to T'Olympics that Never Happened ... or Did It?

The organisers of T'Olympics were very keen that the monarch, Queen Victoria, should pay a visit to the events; they knew that prestige would accrue from this royal seal of approval, and the organisers wrote to the Queen several months before T'Games to try and persuade her to open T'Games or at least attend for one or two days.

Sadly, in an ill-judged 'joke', the initial letter was sent in a kind of mock-stately Yorkshire which it was mistakenly felt would make Victoria curious enough to speed north:

*Heyop, thi Queenliness!*
*Does tha fancy a visit to t' greatest county*
*i' thi Queendom? Does tha fancy t' bracing air*

o' Yorkshire and t' even moor bracing sight o'
many o' thi subjects running an' jumping an'
catching puddings? I bet tha does! Get thissen
up here sharpish! We've got trains an' all
sooarts! Bring Bert if tha wants! Tha'll have
a reyt grand time!

Hey, here's a thowt — tha can oppen it if
tha wants! Brek a bockle o' best Tyke Ale ovver
t' running track!

What sez thi?
Thine,
T'Committee o' T'Olympics.'

After a few weeks T'Committee received a
reply which was cutting in its vagueness:

Her Majesty thanks you for your kind letter. Her
Majesty currently has no plans to visit Exeter.

Undeterred, T'Committee tried again, this time
in standard if somewhat obsequious English:

Gracious Majesty,
If any servants of yours are more humble than

*those in your beloved Yorkshire then please
introduce them to us and we will make ourselves
more humble than those hitherto most humble
subjects of yours. Our knees grow calluses from
bending, our hearts become rickety because we
endlessly pour them out to you.*

*We humbly, humbly request that Your Majesty
loans us the use of one quarter-inch of her Royal
ear as we make a beseeching and humbly
humbling humble request:*

*Would Your Gracious Majesty deem it within
herself to make a brief visit to Your Most Loyal
County to attend a humbly humble and
humblingly humbliferuous sporting event
which we Tykes in our primitive and endearing
way call T'Olympics.*

*We would be able to feed Your Gracious
Majesty with endless portions of Humble Pie
and accommodate Your Gracious Majesty in the
Royal Suite of the Dog and Duck which will be
renamed for your visit the Stag and Swan.*

*In a Humble way we Humbumblingly
Humbleesishly Beseech your Very Most Very
Gracious Very Majesty of Majestiness to consider*

*visiting our most loyal but Humblingly Humble games.*

*T'Committee*

T'Committee received another opaque and oblique reply.

*Dear Mr. T. Committee,*

*Her Majesty thanks you for your letter. She rarely eats pies although yours sound nice. She has no plans to visit the Isle of Man.*

That could have been the end of the matter, but news had leaked out that T'Committee were inviting Queen Victoria to t'Olympics and excitement spread. The Bunting Mill at Bunting Mill near New Mill took on thirty-five new workers, and began to churn out several different sizes and grades of bunting with the royal image on it. Interest in t'Olympics which had hitherto been a little lukewarm or grudging (as is the Yorkshire way) began to blossom.

T'Committee, frankly, panicked. If it turned out that the Queen didn't visit T'Olympics, the

We are not amused

consequences could be dire in terms of public disgruntlement which could eventually lead to public disorder.

So T'Committee came up with a bold if impractical idea: they would employ Obadiah 'Lady' Micklethwaite, a Huddersfield-based female impersonator, to play the part of the Queen. They approached Obadiah and he agreed to do the job if they would pay him in advance in gin. In a move that proved, in hindsight, to be foolhardy, they agreed.

It was announced that the Queen would visit the main site of T'Olympics a couple of weeks before the games to check on the preparation, one Thursday morning at 11am, having caught a special coach from That London, and that she would be making a visit to the Bunting Mill at Bunting Mill.

On the morning in question, cheering crowds lined the (admittedly few) streets of the village of Bunting Mill. There was huge excitement as the royal coach approached, although, in the words of one local "It doesn't look very royal", which wasn't surprising as it was actually Farmer Hidson's Patented Hay Transporter decorated to look royal. In the back sat Obadiah 'Lady' Micklethwaite, dressed in what he fondly imagined the Queen would wear: A pink sack-like dress with a home-made crown. Empty gin bottles rattled in the bottom of the coach.

The coach arrived at the Bunting Mill. T'Chairman of T'Committee was to meet 'the Queen', but she met him when she stumbled out of the coach singing her self-penned song 'I'm the Queen so I Can do What I Want'. The crowd gasped in horror and reeled back. 'The Queen' gave the chairman a slobbering kiss. The crowd shouted in fear and began to move away, some running, some stumbling. Several members of T'Committee wrestled Obadiah back into the coach and he was hustled away, shouting "Put me down or I'll abdicate!"

Several members of T' Committee resigned and the matter was never spoken of again. Not in public anyway.

## Suggestions to T'Committee for Banners to be Displayed during T'Olympics

There's gold in them there Dales!

Ready, steady, go to t'Olympics in Yorkshire!

I run therefore I am tired!

It's not the winning, it's the beating
the others that counts!

They'd nivver have thought o' this
anywhere else!

This is better than working!

Always keep the winning tape in your sights
except when you're not racing!

Put your pumps on the right feet!

It's a marathon not a sprint
— unless it's a sprint!

A healthy mind in a healthy body
is a good idea in theory!

# Yorkshire Pudding Putt

***The history of the event***

The sport began in the yard of the Pig's Arms, Muker, somewhere in the early nineteenth century. The local turnip farmer Simpson Mason enjoyed his beer and always went to the Pig's Arms on a Sunday lunchtime to drink fifteen pints of ale.

Because of this, and because he insisted on singing to the other drinkers from printed broadsheet ballads in an early and primitive version of karaoke, he was always late for his Sunday dinner. These were old-fashioned times: his long-suffering wife Cynthia would make his Yorkshire puddings each week to be crisp and ready from the oven at the time he said he'd be home, and because he was always late they were always burned and dry and sad.

One week her patience ran out in spectacular fashion. They lived in a cottage about five hundred yards from the Pig's Arms and, at the allotted time for Simpson to return, Cynthia filled a Yorkshire pudding with gravy and hurled it from the cottage's back yard in the general direction of the pub.

As luck would have it, Simpson was standing just in the doorway. The pudding whizzed through the air like a meteor or an avenging angel … a gravy-filled meteor/avenging angel. It struck Simpson on the head, concussing him, and all the gravy ran down his best smock because, by some miraculous interface of gravity and centrifugal force, none of the gravy had left the pudding during the short domestic flight.

When he recovered, Simpson became a new man and was always on time for his Sunday dinner and sometimes even cooked it himself.

But the incident had an even more profound effect on the village of Muker. An

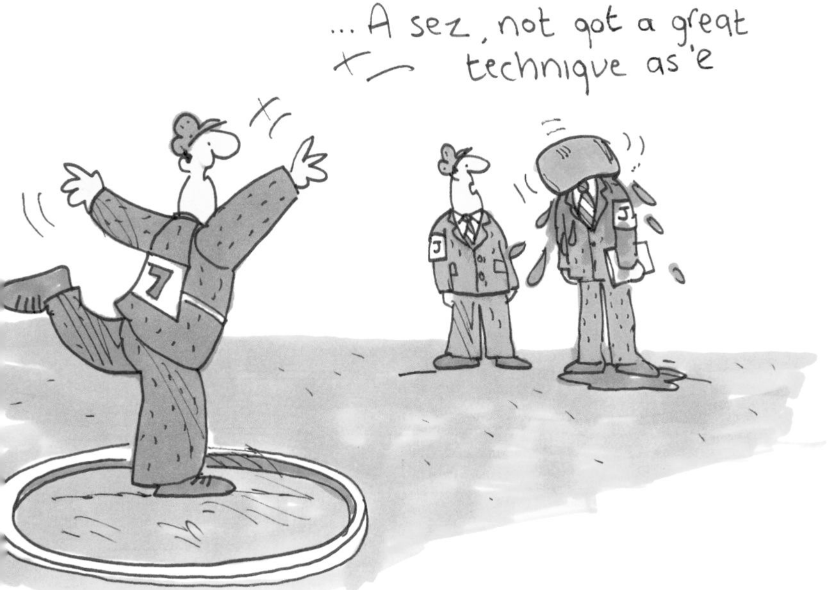
... A sez, not got a great technique as 'e

annual Pudding Putt was established, and eventually competitors from all over the country came to take part, as well as thousands of spectators. Puddings would have to be hurled from the back garden of the Mason dwelling and they would have to land in the yard of the Pig's Arms without losing any gravy.

Over many years, the occasional putter putted the pud into the right spot but they always lost gravy; sometimes all of it, usually most of it. It seemed that Cynthia had a wrist so flexible and strong that, once she hurled the pudding, the gravy would always stay in place.

The Yorkshire Pudding Putt felt like a natural event for T'Olympics and Cynthia, now in advanced old age, agreed to present the medals.

### How it is played

A fifteen-inch circumference Yorkshire pudding is used for the Pudding Putt; the competitor or Pud-Putter has to stand on a circle and the pudding has to be putt from the shoulder.

In essence the sport is a combination of the discus and the shot putt, because the idea is to throw the pudding as far as you can like a shot putt, and the pudding is round like a discus.

The main variation with the Yorkshire Pudding Putt is that the pudding is full of gravy and the Putter scores points not only for the distance the pudding travels but also for the amount of gravy spilled. Obviously the less spillage the more chance of a medal.

# Lancashire Breakfast Mocking

*History of the event*

In 1883, Ebenezer Mason sent his son Moses to have a week at his cousin's farm in Rawtenstall. The idea was that young Moses would help out on the farm at harvest time in return for his bed and board.

After two days a bedraggled and weeping Moses appeared at Ebenezer's door. The conversation reputedly went like this:

Ebenezer: Now then, lad, what are you doing home?

Moses: At breakfast they had a hairnet ovver t' sugar! They had things they called Eccles Cakes and Chorley Cakes! They had a funny platform under t' cup of tea. I can't remember what they called it now...

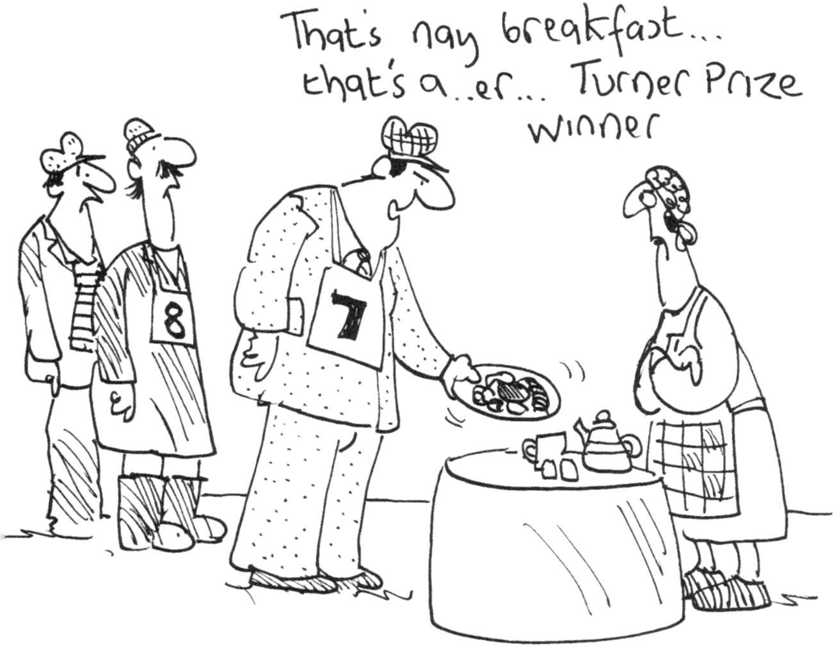
That's nay breakfast...
that's a ..er... Turner Prize
winner
8
7

Ebenezer: A saucer?

Moses: Sosser! That were it! And they cut the crusts off their bread! Doesn't that hurt the bread, dad? And they take the hairnet off the sugar and then they have pickup things to pick the sugar up 'cos the sugar's in lumps! Doesn't the sugar get scared, dad?

Ebenezer: Now don't you worry your head about that, son. Come in and have a cup of hot lard and half a burnt sausage. That'll make you feel a lot better.

Moses: Hairnets ovver t' sugar, dad!

Ebenezer: Shush now. Come on, shush…

### *How it is played*

A Lancashire Breakfast is laid out on a table in front of the competitors. It consists of all the aberrations that Moses saw on his visit to Rawtenstall: Eccles Cakes, Chorley Cakes, the Saucer, the Hairnet over the Sugar Bowl, the Bread With the Crusts Cut Off.

Competitors have to laugh uproariously at the Lancashire Breakfast, and the one who laughs loudest and longest is declared the winner.

# Sherlock Holmes
# and the Missing Quoit

*An extract from a hitherto unpublished Sherlock Holmes story set at the time of T'Olympics.*

"Why the brown study, Holmes?" Dr John Watson asked as the train they were on sped through the dark and smoky Yorkshire townscape. Holmes stretched like a cat.

"I feel that I'm missing something really obvious, my dear Watson," he replied, "but who would ever want to steal a quoit? They are of no practical use to anyone…"

He leaned back on his seat and carried on looking out of the window. It was true that the Quoit Knockout at T'Olympics was in grave danger unless our intrepid and unorthodox hero and his vegetable-like companion could solve the crime and retrieve the goods.

The only other occupant of our compartment appeared to be asleep. Indeed at first sight he appeared to be a bundle of rags that someone had left on the train by mistake. Then, just as we exited a tunnel and rolled into yet another village dominated by a coal mine, the rags spoke, because there was a small, dull-eyed man beneath them.

"They want to keep warm, of course," the man said, apropos of nothing.

Holmes ignored him and began to play his violin. I lit my pipe.

"Are tha listening?" the voice repeated. "Ah reckon they want to keep warm."

Of course he said something like "keeip warrum" but I won't attempt to render his rough patois in print. Holmes stopped playing, halfway through Peronelliellielli's Pavane no 34.

"What on earth are you talking about, sir?" he asked, his voice rising in exasperation.

"I'll tell thi summat," the man said, gesturing

to his rags, "these aren't nicked coyts. Them's found coyts. But I'll tell thi what…"

He leaned closer to Holmes and I saw the great man flinch away, although his breeding prevented him from grimacing; the man's breath was like a fight to the death in a sewer.

"…if I had nicked 'em I'd have nicked for just one reason — to keep warm. That's why tha'd pinch a coyt. Heat. Warmth. Pure and simple. That's what tha wants a coyt for."

Holmes and I got off the train at the next station, and left the man muttering and gesturing.

"How could a quoit keep you warm?" Holmes asked, and I swear I have no answer to that.

# T'Olympics Souvenirs Now Lost

T'Olympics is credited by historians of marketing with the creation of the first sporting souvenirs. A few survive in T'Olympics Wing of the British Museum, but most are lost, including these three frankly ridiculous souvenir ideas:

**T'Olympic Unsmashable Mirror.** Created to celebrate the so-called 'unsmashable' record set by the Drighlington Ladies who crocheted six hundred teapot covers in an hour and which was broken on the first day of T'Olympics by the Halifax Ladies who crocheted seven hundred teapot covers in half an hour, then repaired to the Nag's Head where they crocheted several hundred beer mats and a piano stool. Most of the 'unsmash-able' souvenir mirrors were subsequently smashed, either in anger or delight, or in the case of the mirror belonging to the Rev Harry Greacen, a chess accident.

**T'Olympics Soup.** An early version of Cup-a-Soup which was, perhaps unwisely, made from a distillation of natural but highly unusual Yorkshire ingredients, including 'Yorkshire Soil', 'Watter from a Ditch', 'Smooak from t' Vicar's Pipe' and 'Bits from the Ledge of my Auntie's Hovel'. The three people who tried it were hospitalised for a week, and all sachets were thrown into Gridley Pond, killing all the newts.

**T'Olympics Flag O' Paper.** A souvenir paper flag showing the Union Flag intertwined with the White Rose but which was made of such flimsy tissue-like paper that, as soon as they were placed on the stall, they blew away. Reports of parts of a flag being blown to Belgium were unsubstantiated.

# T' Fastest Yorkshireman Alive

Eric 'what kept yer?' Snowball has the great distinction of being the fastest Yorkshireman who ever lived, but has the lesser distinction of never winning any medals or having any of his great feats of speed propelled by his speedy feet recorded in record books.

The reason is that he was simply too fast. He would stand at the starting line and then appear at the finishing line dusting off his shorts but, oddly, no time would have apparently elapsed. Nobody would have seen him running because he ran faster than the human eye could calculate. Primitive cameras were set up but they'd only catch the moment of setting off and the moment of dusting off.

Conspiracy theories abounded: he was

twins; he had invented some kind of robot or automaton; he was propelled on wheels; he was lying.

Eric naturally took part in all the running races in T'Olympics but was disqualified as he'd finished them all (including T'Marathon) before the rest of the runners had started.

Eric Snowball remains an enigma. I had intended to interview him for this book — but I couldn't catch him.

# BOY FOUND ON ISLAND IN THE ATLANTIC!

## RAN AWAY BECAUSE HE DIDN'T WANT TO RUN

Fishermen landing on remote Itmace Island in the North Atlantic to gather fruit and fresh water, as they did every few years when they passed through that section of the ocean, were surprised to be met by, in the words of Thomas Walkley, the ship's captain, 'A man with a flowing beard and hair as long as a staircase!'

The man turned out to be Jim Jones, who had disappeared from his home in Rotherham shortly before the start of T'Olympics. He had been selected for the 'Three Mile Dash Whilst Carrying Sausages' but had been overcome by nervousness because of his fear of failure.

'He's always been a winner' his mother Alice said, 'and he couldn't live with the idea of dropping his sausages halfway through!'

Jim had sneaked out of Rotherham in the dead of night, walked to the coast and had stowed away on a ship that was bound for New York from Cleethorpes. The crew discovered Jim after a few days and clapped him in irons. He managed to escape, swam away from the boat and ended up on Itmace.

In the end, the supreme irony was that the race never happened because Jim was to have been the only entry. It was replaced by the Bacon Leap, at which Jim would have excelled!

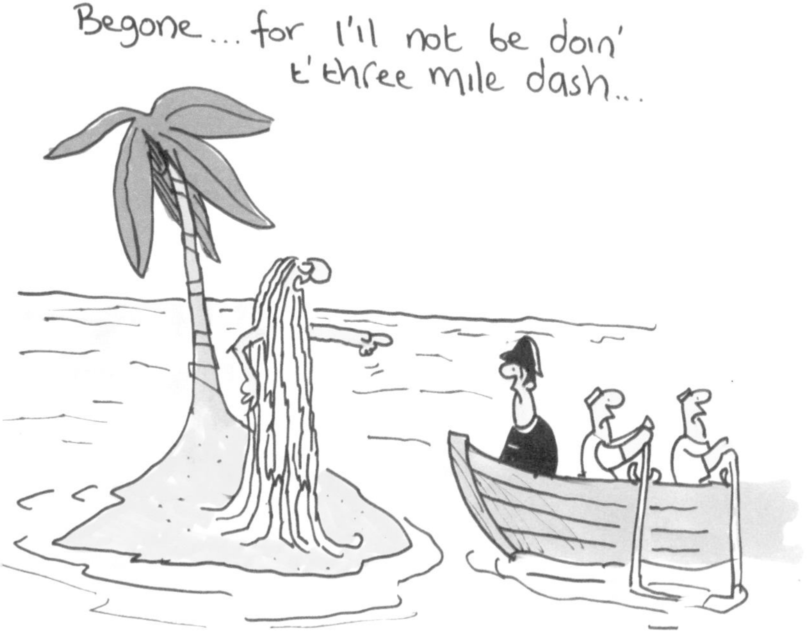
Begone... for I'll not be doin' t'three mile dash...

## *Yorkies Running and Jumping: The Musical*

In 1924 the Yorkshire composer Howard French and the equally Yorkshire lyricist Herbert Browne-Greene were, to put it frankly, down on their luck. They had written hundreds of songs in five years but very few of them had been taken up by the many music publishers who flourished in Tin Pan Alley at the time. Who now remembers their minor novelty hit 'Walk Me To The Cliffs But Don't Chuck Me Over', or their sentimental love song 'My Cheeks Were Designed By An Architect With Drainpipes for My Tears', or their unsuccessful children's opera 'There's No Such Bloke as Father Christmas'.

One day French came across a reference in a newspaper to T'Olympics, an event which, though notorious at the time, had "slipped below memory's radar", to quote the historian Carl Bronson. French and Browne-Greene were immediately fired up: they were both sure that this would make a subject for the hit musical they longed to create for decades.

They set to work, creating a story, familiar now but unusual then, of a team that was expected to have no chance but eventually triumphed.

They invented a team who were taking part in the event known as Getting Thyssen Up Them Stairs (see page 96 for more details of this event). In the musical the team consisted of a number of very elderly people who were initially given no chance of getting up the stairs but, in the tradition of feel-good musicals, finally made it to the gold medal. French and Browne-Greene also introduced a love element, making the Chief Climber a character called Storm Jutson and the Race Starter a lady called Mary Pure.

Convinced that the musical was going to be a success, French and Browne-Greene sank all their savings into the financing of the show, booking a three-week run at the Lyceum Theatre in London's theatreland.

They wrote songs including the rousing opening piece 'Come Up Here and See Some Yorkies Running And Jumping', the tender love song 'I Love You More Than I Love My Mam' and the comedy number 'I Can See Your Vest Under Your Running Shirt'.

The opening night was a triumph — but for all the wrong reasons; as the Times reviewer commented:

"This musical is the worst I have ever seen, but for that reason it is also the best I have ever seen. Come and marvel at the awful tunes and terrible rhymes while there is still time…"

*Yorkies Running and Jumping* became a 'succès fou' as the Germans say; crowds fought to get in and laugh as loudly as they could at the naïve and ridiculous antics being performed on the stage.

Initially shocked, French and Browne-Greene became resigned to the growing reputation of the show as a terrible spectacle following their trousering of the first week's takings.

All would have ended happily were it not for the arrival of a shabbily dressed woman at the theatre one night two-weeks into the run. She looked somehow odd in the opulent surroundings but, as she had a ticket, she was allowed in.

Halfway through the second act, during a quiet period in the aria 'I Came Here For A Silver But I've Found the Gold of Love', the women stood up and announced to the stunned crowd:

"I am Mary Pure and I object to the way I am being portrayed in this travesty!"

There was uproar in the theatre. Mary Pure was rushed from the building but returned the next night with a placard and several burly friends.

Unlike the harridan in the show, the real Mary Pure was a beautiful woman who had been happily married for many years and who had attended T'Olympics out of a love of sport.

French and Browne-Greene were appalled. They tried to buy her off, but Mary's husband was a lawyer and they threatened to sue the composer and lyricist unless the show was curtailed immediately.

French and Browne-Greene had no choice but to end the musical's run and pay Mary all the money they had earned.

It's not known how the name of a real person ended up being used in a piece of fiction but it must have been the case that Browne-Greene had read about Mary in an account of T'Olympics and the name had stuck.

French and Browne-Greene died in poverty. Their example must be a lesson to all creative people that "real life is only a step behind us all", as historian Carl Bronson also said.

# Songs from the Show

Three choruses from the 1924 musical *Yorkies Running and Jumping*.

'Come Up Here and See Some Yorkies Jumping'

> Oh, what's that sound I can hear
> In my trembling ear
> That sets my heart a-thumping
> And gets my blood a-pumping?
> Why, it's…
> Yorkies Running and Jumping
> Yorkies Running and Jumping
> Come up here
> And you will hear
> Ever so clear
> Yorkies running and Jumping!

SONGS FROM THE SHOW

## 'I Love You More
## Than I Love My Mam'

You're a faster runner than she is
You can chuck things further too
Oh you are my medal winner
And you're younger than her: she's 92!


## 'I Can See Your Vest
## Under Your Running Shirt'

Come on, let's flirt
And say flirtatious phrases
Like 'I can see your vest under your
running shirt'
And 'Your breathing just amazes
Me!'
And then you'll see
We'll get together
In this lovely summery charming
Yorkshire weather!

# Harold Thompson, Oldest Surviving Competitor in T'Olympics

Harold Thompson was born in 1891 and was entered in the Bonny Babby competition in T'Olympics, coming last. He is, at the time of writing, 120 years old and in good health, living in his own house near Barnburgh. This is a transcript of my interview with him:

Ian McMillan: Mr Thompson, good morning. I wonder if you can tell me about your memories of T'Olympics.
Harold Thompson: Eh?
I McM: What. Are. Your. Memories. Of. T'Olympics?
HT: Eh?
I McM: WHAT. ARE. YOUR. MEMORIES. OF. T'OLYMPICS?

HT: Hold on while I switch this thing on. That's better. Now, what were you saying?

I McM: What. Are. Your. Memories. Of. T'Olympics?

HT: Nowt.

I McM: Can you be more specific?

HT: Can't remember owt. I were ony a babby.

I McM: What do you recall about the day itself?

HT: Me memory's fine in general. But I can't recall owt abart that 'cos I were ony a babby.

I McM: Maybe these photos will jog your memory.

HT: He's an ugly beggar.

I McM: It's you.

HT: Is it? Ugly.

I McM: This is you in the competition pram. This is you in the competition compound. This is you being pushed round the compound in the competition pram.

HT: Can't remember none of it. I were ony a babby. Can tha recall owt tha did when tha were a babby? I bet tha can't!

I McM: Actually I have complete recall of

everything that's ever happened to me from the age of three days.

HT: Liar!

I McM: Right then, give me a date. I was born on the 21st January 1956.

HT: The 30th January 1956.

I McM: My mam pushed me down the street in the pram. It was snowing.

HT: Tha could be mekkin' that up!

I McM: Well, you could be making all that up about being in T'Olympics. You could be making it up about being 120 years old!

HT: Who said I was 120 years old? I'm 62.

I McM: Well what about these photos?

HT: I were having thi on! Tha wants me granddad. He's in t' kitchen.

I McM: Well why didn't you say so?

HT: 'Cos I like having a laugh with you daft beggars!

*The interview terminates here.*